Empowering The Cake Entrepreneur

-

Jack's Curated Business Idea

-

Jack Lookman

Empowering The Cake Entrepreneur - Jack's Curated Business Idea

A. Acknowledgement

John Tosin Adekunle is acknowledged for his contribution to this project.

My parents, siblings, children, teachers and others, who have contributed positively to my being, are much appreciated.

My Creator and Sustainer is glorified, for seeing me through different facets of my existence.

Alhamdu lillahi rabbi alAAalameena.

To God be the glory.

B. Dedication

This piece of work is dedicated to all Entrepreneurs and Entrepreneurial minds throughout the world.

C. About the book

This book is one of many in the series, 'Jack's Curated Business Ideas.'

The project is an attempt to share many viable business ideas, to enable interested parties to execute.

If consultancy or collaboration is required, we are glad to offer these.

Audio versions could be found on Social media:

- Youtube

- Facebook

- LinkedIn

- Jack's Empowerment - <u>jacksempowerment.com</u>

- Etc?

D. Aims of the project

- To share viable Curated Business Ideas

- To empower and inspire generations

- To add societal value

- To reduce unemployment

- To monetize

- To create wealth

- To reduce crime

- Etc

E. Connect With Us

Facebook group: Curated Business Ideas

Youtube channel: Curated Business Ideas

Facebook Community - Jack Lookman

TikTok - Jack Lookman

LinkedIn - Olayinka Carew aka Jack Lookman

Jack's Empowerment: jacksempowerment.com

Curated Business Ideas - curatedbusinessideas.com

F. Preamble

Sometimes, as Entrepreneurs, we get drowned in our doings.

We don't take deep breaths, to evaluate and explore improvements and opportunities.

As long as we're making money, we continue the grind, and continue the rat race.

In this book, Jack Lookman is exploring wider opportunities, in a business that's apparently very competitive, with little opportunity for growth.

He looks at the business model as an outsider, and shares tips and tricks, which may add immense value to related Entrepreneurs.

Have a great and insightful read.

Best wishes

Jack Lookman

G. The Collection

We have quite a number of books on Jack's Curated Business Ideas.

Please visit jacklookmanlimited.com for the full list of paperbacks.

We shall also be uploading the content to our blog: curatedbusinessideas.com

You could find the videos on our Social media platforms:

Youtube channel - Curated Business Ideas

Facebook group: Curated Business Ideas

The videos could also be found on our membership site: jacksempowerment.com - search for 'Jack's Curated Business Ideas.'

H. Target Audience

- Entrepreneurial minds
- Entrepreneurial educators
- Cake Entrepreneurs
- Entrepreneurs
- Those seeking opportunities
- Investors
- Collaborators
- Etc

I. Polite requests:

- Take notes
- Capture any latent creative ideas that may come to mind
- Take action
- Leverage similar minds
- Monetize
- Make impact
- Leave a great legacy
- Consult with Jack Lookman as necessary
- Spread the word
- Become an Ambassador to the Jack Lookman brand
- Check out other content by Jack Lookman

1. Introduction

Hello, greetings to one and all. This is Jack Lookman welcoming you to our series, 'Jack's curated business ideas.' Today's topic is *Empowering the Cake Entrepreneur."*

You could find content in different formats on our platforms:

- curatedbusinessideas.com
- amazon.co.uk - (visit jacksempowerment.com for the list)
- jacksempowerment.com
- Youtube channel: Curated Business Ideas
- Facebook group: Curated Business Ideas
- etc.

2. The Inspiration

A friend has been in the business of making cakes for quite a while. In my opinion she hasn't optimized the potential income. This content is an attempt to add value to what she does; financially, impact-fully and entrepreneurially.

3. The Idea

The idea is to create content and explore multiple income streams, to leverage sales funnels, to target high income individuals, to explore best practices, as well as other bits and pieces that could propel her earnings.

4. Becoming Organized

It's important to be organized. This will help immensely, in effectively managing resources, as well as in optimizing income.

An organized entrepreneur may generally expend a fraction of resources that a disorganized entrepreneur, will.

The organized entrepreneur will tend to work very smartly in effecting processes, while the disorganized entrepreneur spends repeated time, energy, and resources going round in circles and may end up working very hard but with little productivity to show for it.

There are so many tools that could help enhance your organization skills.

One of them is 'becoming organized' which you could find at jacksempowerment.com

5. Skills and Aptitudes

Some skills and aptitudes required for the business, include:

• Communication skills
• Interpersonal skills
• Customer services skills

- People management skills
- Entrepreneurial skills
- Cake design and production skills
- Time management skills
- Resource management skills
- Tenacity
- Administrative skills
- Integrity
- Telephone skills
- Hunger for Success
- Marketing skills
- Negotiation skills
- Human resource management skills
- Research and development skills
- Training and development skills
- Etc.

6. Legalities

Some key considerations include:

- Refunds policy
- Cancellation policy
- Research and Development
- Risk management
- Health and safety issues
- Data management, especially relating to General Data Protection Regulation (GDPR) especially for those in Europe.
- Expectation management
- Disclaimers and indemnifications

- Business registration
- Managing litigation
- Staffing issues
- Contracts and agreements
- Terms and conditions
- Etc.

• Concerning legal matters you could either solicit the services of a legal professional, or you could do your research online; the second option could be a lot cheaper and affordable but it's a judgment call for you.

7. Disclaimer and indemnification

This content is an academic exercise and just an idea. Though it has great potential to create wealth, nothing is guaranteed.
Having an idea is just one of many steps to make business and financial success. The expectation is that you shall carry out due diligence, perfect the idea, consult as necessary, seek Divine guidance and help, and then take action.
It is hoped and expected that by you doing all it takes, you could benefit immensely both financially and otherwise.
Just to reiterate "Success is Not Guaranteed."
Jack Lookman and Jack Lookman Limited shall not take responsibility for any financial or other losses.

8. Risk Management

You need to have systems and structures in place to manage risks.
Risks could include:
- accidents— on or off site
- litigation
- conflicts
- unplanned price variations - due to inflation or circumstances out of your control
- reduced business income
- loss of life or sickness
- staff turn around
- accommodation changes
- epidemics
- etc.

- You need to mitigate the risks and have plans a, b and c in anticipation of such eventualities.
- Getting relevant insurance may also be part of your business plan and risk management.

9. Research and Development

The importance of research and development cannot be overemphasized; You need to do:

- Competitor research
  - research best practices and potential pitfalls

- Product research
- Market research
- Etc.

- You could use the outcomes of the above, to improve your value proposition.

10. Competitor Research

You need to research your competitors
- leverage their good practices
- avoid pitfalls
- use their pricing as a guide for yours
- etc.

11. Health and Safety

Be mindful of health and safety implications.
- In the production of cake be mindful of bugs and other health risks.
- Be mindful of hazards from the oven, and in transportation
- Etc.

- Be mindful of possible litigation from unhappy clients, staff and third parties, etc.

12. Marketing

- This is a very important part of the business.
- You could either do in-house marketing house, by yourself, or you could outsource it to freelancers or necessary others.

- You could explore the use of SEO (search engine optimisation)

- You could use:
  - digital marketers
  - social media marketers
  - influencer marketers
  - print marketers
  - television marketers
  - radio marketers
  - WhatsApp marketing
  - telegram marketing
  - email marketing
  - etc

  - You need to have a periodic budget for marketing.
- You need to review your marketing efforts regularly, to know what aspects of it are profitable or unprofitable; and to increase or decrease marketing budgets accordingly.
- You also need to have the the mindset that marketing never ends.

- By stopping your marketing efforts you run the risk of your competitors taking advantage; and you losing money. This may even spell the beginning of the end of your business.
- Ensure that you target high income earners who could afford increased charges or prices
- You might also have off-the-shelf products and services for the lower end market.

13. Sales Funnel

As part of your marketing plan, you need to have a sales funnel.
- You need a lead magnet or magnets
- You need upsells, down-sells and cross sells
- You need to optimally monetize your clients.
- Your sale of cakes shall only be a small part of your income. The other bits and pieces that you offer on the sales journey may be what increases your income from tens of thousands of pounds to may be hundreds of thousands of pounds.
- You may decide to market related products and services which your client demographic or client avatar may find of interest.
- You may continue to market and re-market products and services to your clients in coming months, years and decades.
- The products and services that you market, may be yours, as well as those of third parties.

14. Automation

It may be crucial to automate your processes. This could give you a competitive advantage.

- Automation may involve the use of artificial intelligence as a complementary resource for your content creation.
- You may automate your marketing and publicity efforts.
- You may leverage automation with social media.
- You may leverage automation on your WhatsApp platform.
- You may automate your process for taking orders.
- You may automate your administrative processes.

- By automating or semi automating, you could also free up time and resources which you could therefore use on other important activities.

15. Financial Matters

You need to give consideration to the following:

- Budgeting
- Staff salaries (as necessary)
- Capital costs
- Running costs
- Equipment purchase
- Administrative costs
- Business registration

- Maintenance of equipment
- Website hosting
- Website domain costs
- Business administration costs
- Business accounting
- Cake production
- Cake transportation to the client (and logistics)
- Risk management
- Unexpected costs
- Energy costs
- Insurance costs
- Research and development
- Training and development
- Loans and repayments
- Government taxes
- Miscellaneous costs
- Unplanned costs

- You also need to do your costing and pricing effectively, because this could make or mar your business.

16. Funding options

These could include:

- crowdfunding
- self funding
- business loans
- investors

- family and friends
- collaborators
- etc

17. Budgeting

Is there a need for budgeting?

Yes, there is. This shall give clarity to your requirements. It shall also give a more practical and realistic insight to the business. You'll have an idea of how much you require periodically. You could effectively plan. You could effectively manage resources.

If you require funding, budgeting becomes very handy.

The budget shall guide your activities; it shall also make you more organized. It helps you prioritize and helps you get the best out of your business.

18. Business Registration

You need to consider your options; whether to be a sole trader, a limited liability company, or whether your business should be a joint venture, etc.

Each of these options have pros and cons.

Please research the internet and contact relevant others before deciding on the path to journey.

Most entrepreneurs start as sole traders, before progressing to become limited liability companies.

Technically speaking, you need to register your business before trading; however most people test the waters by starting to trade, before embarking on business registration.

19. Human Resources and Work Streams

Some considerations are:

• Manager
• Entrepreneur
• Customer services
• IT professional
• Marketer
• Administrator
• Strategist
• Researcher
• Logistics
• Baker
• Social media manager.

• Multiple roles could be played by the same individual.

20. Income Streams

These shall include:

• Baking and selling cake in different niches; this could include:
    • party cakes
    • wedding cakes
    • birthday cakes
    • celebration cakes
    • cup cakes
    • graduation cakes
    • matriculation cakes
    • etc.

• Mentoring and coaching is another income stream that you could explore.
• You could teach others what you do.
• This could be accomplished online, offline or both.

• You could create online courses:
    • this could include video, text, or audio formats.
    • And could be on different platforms such as YouTube, Facebook, Social Media, membership site, blog, podcast, paperback, ebook, etc.

- You could include links to your other products and services, as well as links to third party products and services.
    - Third parties could include others in the industry.
    - You could promote equipment, event planners, mentors and coaches.
    - You could even promote selected competitors.
    - You could monetize via adverts, sponsorships or affiliate marketing.
    - You could promote relevant digital products and services.
    - You could create a mailing list and promote products and services to them for a lifetime.
    - You could promote products and services to parents, for themselves and their children.
    - You could promote related products and services also to your clients who are professionals.

    - You could promote products and services accordingly to your clients who have entrepreneurial minds.
    - You could promote products and services accordingly for those who are migrants.
    - You could do likewise for those seeking career changes.
    - You could do the same for those seeking investment opportunities.
    - You could actually market and re-market different product services to your audience or to your clients.

- You also need to increase the price of your value proposition. You might increase your price by x% or as necessary.
- As part of your marketing efforts, you need to target clients who could afford your prices.

21. Affiliate Marketing

You could approach affiliate marketing via two means. You could be an affiliate marketer for other brands or you could create your own affiliate marketing platform.

By being an affiliate marketer for other brands, you could do so passively or actively. You could promote their products and services on your platforms and get a commission for each sale made.

If you decide to offer affiliate marketing for your brand, you could encourage your clients and necessary others, to promote your brand, products and services, in return for an agreed commission.

22. Platforms

You could leverage different platforms for your business. They shall be for marketing, for sharing your value proposition, for information purposes and for monetization.

You could have a YouTube channel, a Facebook group, a Facebook page, a blog, a podcast, a membership site and relevant other social media platforms, etc.

Some of these come at a cost, while others are free.

These could be reference points for your value offers, they could also help build trust and confidence in you and your business.

For the social media platforms, you need to know the platforms where your target demographics generally hang out.

That way, you could target them effectively. You need to upload quality relevant content as necessary, and you need to be responsive.
If you decide to have a membership site, this could accommodate mentoring and coaching content and be a useful platform for sharing knowledge, experience and impact. It's an opportunity to share content over and above your cake proposition.

You could create a community, and get them to pay as necessary, to access the membership site periodically. So for all intents and purpose, if they want to access your membership site for just one month, 6 months and maybe one year, etc; you could charge them accordingly; and this process is actually automated on the membership site;
You could also upsell, down sell, and cross sell other products and services.

At Jackman Lookman Limited, the platform we use Member Vault.

We could help build your membership site if interested.

Please visit 'Business Collaboration With Jack Lookman,' this can be found at jacksempowerment.com. Our membership site is called 'Jack's Empowerment.'

23. E-mail Marketing

In the process of offering your products and services, it's good practice to collect and monetize contact details. This shall be done by email marketing. You shall continually compile a mailing list; it could include the name of your client, the mobile number, the email address, etc. Armed with this list, you could market products and services of yourself and others, for as long as possible. You however need to be mindful of legal implications, such as GDPR (General Data Protection Regulation in Europe), etc.

24. Content Creation

Content could be in form of videos, audio, text, or a combination. It could be on multiple platforms, for example blogs, YouTube, Facebook, social media, membership sites, ebooks, paperbacks, etc.

For cake related content, ideas could include:

- videos of you baking the cake
- purchase of raw ingredients for baking the cake
- collaborative content on your platforms or links to such; this could include content on:
  - Family Matters
  - Education
  - Spirituality
  - Mindfulness
  - Relationships
  - Business monetization
  - Health and well-being
  - Etc.

  - You could monetize this directly or as an affiliate marketer.

25. Is it a good idea to create videos?

Short engaging videos are particularly attractive to most people.

In my opinion, I would say you could create videos on you curating the cake, on you purchasing the ingredients, on you doing your administration, on you delivering the cake to happy clients. This could build trust and confidence in your potential and existing clients

This could also nudge them to patronize you even more. You however need to be mindful of legal implications.

The videos shall come in handy for your digital platforms as well as for your mentees.

You need to be mindful of sharing sensitive trade secrets.

26. Types of Cakes

You could have cupcakes, birthday cakes, event cakes. You could have cakes for naming ceremonies, for weddings and for send-offs. You could have graduation cakes, etc.

27. Suggested Digital Platforms

Some useful digital platforms include:

- YouTube
- Facebook
- TikTok
- Instagram
- Social media (others)
- Blogs
- Podcast
- Membership sites
- Ebooks

- Websites
- Whatsapp
- Telegram
- Etc.

28. Work streams

These shall include:

- Baking
- Logistics
- Shopping
- Customer services
- Social media management
- Information technology
- Cake design
- Management
- Human Resources
- Marketing
- Strategizing and brainstorming
- Research and development
- Training and development
- Administration
- Customer service
- Etc.

29. Is Customer Service Important?

It is of very great importance. The way you offer customer service says a lot about your business.

- This could range from the way you treat your clients and third parties over the phone, over the internet, and in person.
- Whether you are courteous and professional.
- Whether you are rude and unhelpful.
- Whether you resolve areas of concern and conflict; and in a timely manner.
- How your digital platforms are portrayed to the outside world.
- Whether your platforms are user-friendly.
- Whether you keep to your promises.
- Whether your sole concern is just profit, as opposed to the value given.
- Whether your clients will be glad to market and re-market your brand.
- Whether your customers are repeat customers.
- Whether you have a long-lasting positive relationship with your customers.
- Whether the reviews on your platforms are very positive.
- Whether you listen to suggestions and feedback from your clients and customers and whether you act on them.
- Etc.

30. Are There Benefits in Collaborating?

Collaboration could be a two-edged sword. It may, or may not work for you. Though you may carry out due diligence, it's sometimes a case of trial and error.
If you get it right, and pick the right collaborators, it could do you immense good. You could share resources; you could share thoughts and experiences, you could share best practices, etc, for the common good. If you however get the wrong collaborators, you may waste resources continually, you may conflict regularly, and make little or no business progress. Therefore, if you wish to have collaborators, give it a lot of thought, carry out due diligence, and have a trial period for a period, before committing to any long-term relationship. You might back the collaboration with legal documents, and include exit clauses.

31. Training & Development

As you probably know, the world has become extremely fast paced, with lots of competition.
People and businesses are becoming more efficient. It shall be a great understatement to express the need for training and development.
It is an important variable in the business space if you wish to be competitive. The possible consequences

of not investing in training and development, is that the train of success and profit could leave you behind. You need to invest in training and development for yourself and for your team on a regular basis, or as necessary.

Learn from best practices, avoid pitfalls, and share knowledge and experiences with team members regularly in order to minimize the cost of training and development. You may consider leveraging digital courses. This may effectively complement your practical training; the training may be in-house or external. The training and development shall be in different aspects that relate to your business such as customer services, baking, health and safety, legalities, etc. There are loads of courses on platforms such as Youtube (youtube.com), Udemy (udemy.com), etc. For a free guide on the use of Udemy, please visit jacksempowerment.com .

32. Is Mindset Important?

In my opinion mindset is indeed a big deal. It could be the foundation of success or failure.
With the right positive mindset, you could literally move mountains and achieve success. Whereas with the wrong mindset, you could actually fail before beginning.
Your mindset is your perception of things and events.

A person with a negative mindset could see problems, pain, and doom; whereas a person with a positive mindset could see opportunity, prosperity, and impact.

You could decide on the crowd to surround yourself, with, and decide on whether investments in mindset courses and activities could benefit you, your team, and your business; in the short and long term.

Apart from yourself, you need to work on the mindset of your staff; if they have questionable mindsets, this could translate into negative relations with your customers, poor performance, and therefore impact sales negatively.

33. Rewards And Sanctions

You could give rewards, sanctions and incentives, as necessary. These could go to your staff, clients, or necessary others.

By rewarding them, there are chances that they they'll multiply the goodness that they offer; and this could result in a win-win for all.

Rewards could be in form of digital or physical gifts. It could in the form of recognition, promotion, one-off financial gift, pay increase, etc, for your staff.

It could also be in the form of a surprise gift, training and development, etc.

For clients, these could include discounts, recognition (maybe thank-you-cards), complimentary gifts, company souvenirs, gift cards, etc.

On the other hand, there could be sanctions for poor or negative practices by the clients. You may terminate business relations with them; there might also be fines for bad behavior or negative attitudes, or possible legal action.

Whereas for staff it might be termination, suspension or demotion, etc.

34. Opportunities

By embarking on this business model, you would be opening yourself to different opportunities.
These include:
- networking
- monetisation
- business growth
- collaborative opportunities
- better quality of life
- making societal impact
- learning opportunities
- multiple income streams
- job creation
- wealth creation
- legacy projects
- etc

35. Business Requirements

These could include:

- cake-making equipment
- a location
- relevant skills
- Human Resources
- digital devices
- internet connection
- entrepreneurial mindset
- growth mindset
- cake delivery logistics
- transportation
- energy supply, e.g. electricity or gas
- etc.

36. Complementary products and services

Apart from the cake which is your main product, you could also explore other sub-niches.
- You could explore other sub niches in that industry.
- You could explore cake for different events.

- You could explore affiliate marketing for products and services in that industry, for example equipment, logistics, training and development, etc.
- You could create complimentary content on your doings and experience.
- You could have a sales funnel, marketing and re-marketing relevant products and services to your mailing list; via email marketing and affiliate marketing.
- You could collaborate with third parties
- You could do public speaking.
- You could mentor interested persons.
- You could have a monetized membership site.
- You could have a monetized blog.
- You could have social media platforms, for example YouTube, Facebook, Instagram, etc.
- You could have a podcast.
- You could have an app.
- You could have a cake shop.
- You could have a franchise.
- You could do event planning and execution.
- You could have monetized adverts on your digital platforms.
- If you are of Nigerian heritage, you might explore being in the value chain for products such as:
    - Chin-Chin
    - Puff-puff
    - Jollof rice
    - Suya
    - Meat pie
    - Etc.

- You could also organize cake and food competitions.
- You could facilitate <u>freelance domestic culinary coaching</u>, and by the way we have a video on that. So, if you search for *Freelance Domestic Culinary Coaching* by Jack Lookman, you could find that on YouTube and <u>Facebook</u>.

37. Targets

Most businesses that thrive, set achievable targets; the targets may be financial, they may be performance targets, sales targets, targets on customer retention, number of positive reviews, or targets on social media interactions, etc. Targets generally motivate performance; they are measurable and could help you improve on the value that you offer.

38. Business Processes

You may want to consider the undermentioned. They are not ordered in any format or chronology. They are just suggestions. These could include:

- baking the cake
- purchasing ingredients
- getting organized

- marketing and publicity
- team meetings
- social media management
- IT management
- automation of processes (as necessary)
- collaboration
- staff management
- administration
- payment of salaries (on time)
- training and development
- research and development
- customer services
- strategizing
- brainstorming
- logistics
- content creation
- etc.

39. Conclusion

In conclusion here are some thoughts to ponder.

- We are all growing old by the day.
- We are not as strong as we used to be.
- Pensioners are generally poor.
- Could you make hay while the sun shines?
- Could you explore passive residual and multiple income streams while you can?

- There are no longer jobs for life like they used to be.
- The younger ones and robots may threaten your job.
- You could effectively leverage the internet and other resources to achieve your goals.
- You could leverage mentors and necessary others.
- Pricing and costing are of great importance.
- You could become wealthy.
- You could <u>Book A Chat With Jack Lookman</u> for greater insight.

These are some food for thought.

40. Did you get any value?

We hope that you learnt one or two things. If so, please consider spreading the word.
- You could like, share, subscribe, repost, and comment on our different social media platforms.
- You could share our blogs.
- You could purchase our many books.
- Please visit <u>jacklookmanlimited.com</u> for the list and links to our various books, products and services.
- If you require mentoring and coaching from Jack Lookman, please visit Jack's Mentoring 101 (you can find this at <u>jacksempowerment.com</u>)

- If you wish to collaborate with Jack Lookman, please visit Business Collaboration With Jack

Lookman. You could find this at jacksempowerment.com.

- Do you wish to learn more about Jack Lookman? If so, please join his Facebook Community at Jack Lookman.
- At Jack Lookman Limited we offer a range of services. We could also help set up your membership site as well as social media platforms, and to brainstorm with you.
- Do you wish to collaborate with Jack Lookman?
- Do you wish to learn more about this, or other ideas?
- If so, please check out Business Collaboration With Jack Lookman at jacksempowerment.com
- Also, feel free to visit jacklookmanlimited.com to see our range of products and services.
- You could explore opportunities to work with Jack Lookman.
- Our products and services include a range of paperbacks and video content on Curated Business Ideas, Mindset, etc.
- We have different blogs and a membership site (jacksempowerment.com).
- We have social media content (please see jacklookmanlimited.com)
- We have a library of videos on Jack's Curated Business Ideas. This can be found at jacksempowerment.com.

- You could also join Jack Lookman's community on Facebook. Search for Jack Lookman on Facebook

- We Create Content
- We Mentor
- We do Affiliate Marketing
- We do Business Collaborations
- And App Development Collaborations

- We've authored and published several books on
  - Curated Business Ideas
  - Mindset
  - Poetry
  - Jaaloo Puzzles
  - Yoruba
  - Life Experience
  - Etc

- If you are interested in playing an arithmetic number game called Jaaloo Puzzles, it's very good brain exercise for children, adults, youths and the elderly. It helps with accuracy skills, mental alertness, competition skills, arithmetic and logic skills. You could find it at jaaloo.com and jaaloopuzzles.com

41. About Jack Lookman Limited

At Jack Lookman Limited, our mission is to Empower and Inspire Generations, by Leveraging the Internet.

We create content, we mentor, we inspire, and we collaborate.

42. About Jack Lookman

Jack Lookman is the director and owner of Jack Lookman Limited. He is a Content Creator, Mentor, Multiple Author, Entrepreneur and Business Collaborator. His background is in Engineering. He worked for several years as an administrator and has lots of experience in paid and unpaid roles.

43. Here are Some Useful Sign Posts

jacksempowerment.com

- Jack's Mentoring 101
- Business Collaboration With Jack Lookman
- Becoming Organized
- Profit Sharing Formula App - Youtube - Facebook - Amazon - curatedbusinessideas.com

- Writing a business plan. You can find that on YouTube and at
  - https://amzn.to/3W2Xuwf
  - https://amzn.to/4bzAQjK
  - https://amzn.to/3XM6p6p

- Curated Business Ideas on our YouTube channel, Facebook group and Facebook Community
- If you want to have access to our blog for free, visit curatedbusinessideas.com
- Freelance domestic culinary coaching: you can find that on Youtube by Jack Lookman.
- Empowering The Cake Entrepreneur - Blog - curatedbusinessideas.com

44. How could Jack Lookman help?

- He could help with creating a membership site as well as creating YouTube and Facebook social media platforms.
- He could assist with brainstorming and exploring different options.
- If interested, please 'Book A Chat With Jack Lookman' just visit jacksempowerment.com

- You can also send an email to info@Jackmanlimited.com

45. Important Notice

At Jack Lookman Limited there are opportunities for investors and collaborators.

46. Feedback

Please forward your feedback to info@jacklookmanlimited.com

47. Disclaimer

We do Affiliate Marketing by promoting products and services. Upon making sales, we get commissions at no additional cost to you.

48. Mission

Our mission at Jack Lookman Limited is to empower and Inspire Generations by leveraging the internet.

49. Useful compliments

1. Jack's Empowerment - membership site - jacksempowerment.com

2. Jaaloo Puzzles - blog - jaaloopuzzles.com - jaaloo.com

3. Curated Business Ideas - blog - curatedbusinessideas.com

4. Jack Lookman Limited - blog - jacklookmanlimited.com

5. Youtube channel: Curated Business Ideas

6. Youtube channel: Jaaloo Puzzles

7. Youtube channel: Life Lessons For Teenagers

8. Facebook: Jack Lookman

9. Facebook: Curated Business Ideas

10. Facebook: Jaaloo Puzzles

11. Facebook: Life Lessons For Teenagers

12. Jack Lookman's Books - jacklookmanlimited.com

13. Business Collaboration With Jack Lookman - jacksempowerment.com

14. Jack's Mentoring 101 - jacksempowerment.com

15. Life Lessons For Teenagers : lifelessonsforteenagers.com

16. Book A Chat With Jack Lookman : jacksempowerment.com

17. TikTok - jacklookman4

18. LinkedIn - Olayinka Carew aka Jack Lookman

19. Yoruba Project - yorubaproject.com

50. Books by Jack Lookman

Visit:

- jacklookmanlimited.com
- Internet search - Jack Lookman
- Jack Lookman's Books
- amazon.co.uk
- reputable book shops (online)

51. Some resources by Jack Lookman

- Jack's Empowerment - jacksempowerment.com
- Jaaloo Puzzles - jaaloopuzzles.com
- Jaaloo Puzzles - Baby Jaaloo - jaaloo.com
- Jaaloo Puzzles - jaaloopuzzles.com
- Jack Lookman Limited: jacklookmanlimited.com
- Curated Business Ideas curatedbusinessideas.com
- Jack's Life Lessons For Teenagers: lifelessonsforteenagers.com
- Youtube channel: Curated Business Ideas
- Youtube channel: Jack's Life Lessons For Teenagers
- Youtube channel: Oro Ishiti- Indelible Yoruba Words

- Youtube channel: Jaaloo Puzzles
- Facebook: Jack Lookman
- Facebook group: Curated Business Ideas
- Facebook group: Menteero
- Facebook group: Jaaloo Puzzles
- Facebook group: Jack's Life Lessons For Teenagers
- Facebook group: Yoruba Project
- Yoruba Project: yorubaproject.com
- Jack's Curated Business Ideas: jacksempowerment.com
- Affiliate Marketing: jacksempowerment.com
- Etc.

52. Will you like to collaborate?

Does the Jack Lookman brand resonate with you? Will you like to collaborate? If yes, please send an email to: info@jacklookmanlimited.com

Use an appropriate subject heading and narrative.

Or search for 'Business Collaboration With Jack Lookman' online.

53. Will you like to be mentored by Jack Lookman?

If yes, please send an email to: info@jacklookmanlimited.com

Use an appropriate subject heading and narrative.

Or search for 'Jack's Mentoring 101' online or at jacksempowerment.com

54. OTHER PUBLICATIONS BY Jack Lookman Limited

1. *Despair, Submission, Faith and Hope – Volume 1*
2. *Despair, Submission, Faith and Hope – Volume 2*
3. *Monetising Digital Book Reviews*
4. *E-Commerce For Traditional African Attires*
5. *Basic Management And Fundraising Tip For Community Groups*
6. *Monetising A Digital Library*
7. *Ajo, The App And Opportunities*
8. *Empowering Orphans, Widows and Widowers*
9. *Submission, Gratitude, Faith and Hope*
10. *Oro Ishiti- Indelible Yoruba Words - Adebanji Osanyingbemi*
11. *Eid Monetisation by Leveraging Technology*
12. *What are your thoughts? What is your mindset? - Volume 1*
13. *What are your thoughts? What is your mindset? - Volume 2*
14. *Twenty Curated Business Ideas - Volume 1*
15. *Jaaloo Puzzles - Volume 1*
16. *Jaaloo Puzzles - Volume 2*
17. *Beauty Of The Storm - Gabriel Adeola*
18. *Digital Career Guidance App*

This is <u>Jack Lookman</u> signing off.

Ire o (I wish you blessings)

Ire kabiti (I wish you loads of blessings).

www.ingramcontent.com/pod-product-compliance
Lightning Source LLC
Chambersburg PA
CBHW072018230526
45479CB00008B/286